Shutterstock/AndreAnita

Scottish Recipes

A selection of traditional Scottish recipes

By **Amanda Wragg**

BRADWELL
BOOKS

1

Published by Bradwell Books

9 Orgreave Close Sheffield S13 9NP

Email: books@bradwellbooks.co.uk

British Library Cataloguing in Publication Data: a catalogue record for this book is available from the British Library.

1st Edition

ISBN: 9781902674810

Print: Gomer Press, Llandysul, Ceredigion SA44 4JL TBC

Artwork and design by: Andrew Caffrey

The photographs used in this book are to illustrate the dish and are not meant as a final representation of the finished result. Any garnish or additions are at your discretion.

Recipes

Introduction

Shutterstock/Jason Vandehey

There was a time not too many years ago when Scotland was something of a culinary desert; nothing could be further from the truth today. Scotland's natural bounty of game, fish and dairy forms the backbone of the vibrant Scottish food map. From the lush, rolling Cheviot Hills on the southern border to the wild, invigorating northernmost reaches on the Atlantic Ocean, Scotland's surprisingly temperate climate yields a tremendous variety of top quality ingredients.

Not only have artisan makers and producers proliferated, but some of the country's best restaurants run by internationally respected chefs can be found north of the border. Given how small it is – only 274 miles long and at its widest point 154 miles – the food offering is extraordinary.

The jagged coastline runs to over 2000 miles so it's no surprise that the seafood is world class, and you'll find a huge variety of vegetables, top quality meat and game and brilliant cheeses put to good use in a number of traditional recipes, many of them to be found here. Start your day with a bowl of hearty porridge, grab a tasty seafood lunch and finish the day with a glass of cranachan; you can eat simply but well any time of the day or year.

As a lifelong visitor and lover of Scottish food, I'm delighted to be able to share some of my favourite recipes; I'm indebted to Shirley Spear of the Three Chimneys, Skye, and Claire MacDonald of Kinloch Lodge for their generous contributions.

Amanda Wragg

Shutterstock/Daniele Carotenuto

Vegetable Stock

Since time immemorial country people the world over have kept the stockpot simmering all day on the kitchen stove. Those days are pretty much gone, but making a good basic stock isn't difficult and although there are many quick options these days (even one or two of our 'top' chefs are advertising stock cubes!) there's nothing as satisfying as knowing your soup, stew or casserole is made with the real deal. This flavoursome stock will last for up to a week in the fridge, or batch freeze it for later use. Many cooks make different stocks depending on what they're the basis of; beef, fish, chicken – but I find this basic stock will do nicely for any dish you're making.

Ingredients

3 medium onions

5 medium carrots

3 medium leeks

3 sticks celery

8 cabbage leaves

Handful flat leaf parsley

3 sprigs fresh thyme

1 bay leaf

Sea salt

3.5 litres cold water

Method

1   Roughly chop the vegetables and put in a large saucepan or stockpot with all the other ingredients.

2   Cover with water and bring slowly to the boil.

3   Reduce the heat to a gentle simmer. Skim off any scum.

4   Simmer very gently with the lid ajar for an hour, skimming from time to time.

5   Strain through a sieve – don't push any of the soft vegetables through as the stock will become cloudy. Allow to cool then refrigerate.

Shutterstock/Ben Smith

Soda Bread

There are many artisan bakers in Scotland, but there is nothing quite like filling the house with the smell of home-baked bread. It is much easier than most people think, especially using the soda bread recipe below; you'll get one largish loaf or three smaller ones. Soda bread tends to be denser than yeasted bread, so don't be surprised if it doesn't rise quite as much as you might expect.

Ingredients

400g wholemeal flour

75g plain white flour (you can use strong bread flour if you have it)

1 tsp salt

1 tsp bicarbonate of soda

1 large egg

1 tbsp vegetable oil of your choice

1 tsp honey, treacle or soft brown sugar, whichever you have to hand

425 ml buttermilk or sour milk*

*To make sour milk, take 425ml milk, add the juice of ½ a lemon, give it a quick stir, leave for 10 minutes and off you go.

Method

1   Preheat the oven to 400F/200oC/gas 6. Prepare a loaf tin (23 x 12.5 x 5cm) by brushing with vegetable oil or lining with a paper liner, or use smaller tins if you prefer.

2   Put the dry ingredients into a large bowl and sieve in the bicarbonate of soda. Mix well.

3   Whisk the egg and then add the oil, sugar/honey/treacle and the buttermilk or sour milk. Make a well in the centre of the dry ingredients and pour in all the liquid. Using a large wooden spoon mix well, scraping the flour from the sides until all the ingredients are blended into a smooth, slightly gloopy mixture. Add more milk if necessary.

4   Pour into the loaf tin(s) and sprinkle on some seeds on top if you fancy (sunflower seeds or linseeds are nice).

5   Put in the oven for an hour and then check to see if the loaf is cooked through using a skewer. If the bread is ready it will sound hollow when you knock it on the bottom, and the skewer should come out clean.

Shutterstock/Lyudmila Suvarova

Porridge

We all have our preferred way of making it; I wouldn't presume to tell you that my way is the best way, but I would advise that the better the oats, the better the result. Sometimes we're short of time in the morning – and there's nothing wrong with making it in a microwave, but for me, standing at the stove, stirring and watching the bubbles is a form of relaxation.

Ingredients SERVES 2

1 cup good quality oats

1 cup skimmed milk

1 cup water

Shutterstock /Thinglass

Method

1   Measure your oats out into a pan. Add the milk and water. Stir the cold ingredients together. Cook for around 10 minutes on a low to medium heat, stirring constantly, until the mix starts to thicken and bubble.

2   Serve with Golden Syrup, salt, jam, honey – or naked. The porridge, not you. My other half sprinkles salt round the outside and puts a blob of jam in the middle. Takes all sorts.

Shutterstock/Jorge Beuge

Omelette

Sometimes the simplest dishes are the best. If you're strapped for time (or cash) a straightforward omelette hits the spot. Some folk are anxious around making them – but don't fear, very little can go wrong! You can ring the changes by adding all sorts: mushrooms, tomatoes or a sprinkling of herbs. The Dunlop Dairy in East Ayrshire makes wonderful cow and goat cheese – you can buy it all over Scotland – their traditional Ayreshire Dunlop works beautifully here.

Ingredients SERVES 1

2 large free-range eggs

Sea salt

Freshly ground black pepper

1 small knob of butter

1 small handful of grated farmhouse cheese

Method

1   Crack the eggs into a bowl with a pinch of salt & pepper. Beat well with a fork. Put a small pan on a low heat and add the butter. When it's melted and starting to bubble, add the eggs, moving them round the pan to spread them out evenly.

2   When the eggs start to firm up but still with a bit of raw on top, sprinkle over the cheese. Ease round the edges of the omelette then fold it over, in half. When it starts to turn golden brown underneath, slide it from the pan onto a plate.

3   Snip some parsley, chives or basil over the top and tuck in with a chunk of home made bread and glass of wine.

Shutterstock/Tatiana Frank

Oat Cakes

These tasty biscuits (or bannocks) are so Scottish they're positively tartan. Easy to make, they're perfect with farmhouse cheese and good chutney. And the smell in the kitchen when you're making them is worth the effort alone. You can use rolled oats, but pinhead oatmeal will produce the real deal.

Ingredients

225g pinhead oatmeal

½ tsp baking powder

50g chilled butter

1 tsp salt

½ tsp granulated sugar

70ml hot water

Method

1   Pre-heat the oven to 190C/Gas 5. In a large bowl mix together the oatmeal, flour, sugar and baking powder. Cut the chilled butter into small pieces and add to the flour. Rub together until you have a consistency of bread crumbs.

2   Add the water bit by bit and combine until you've got a thick dough. Sprinkle some extra flour on a work surface and roll the dough out – about ½ cm thick. Use a cookie cutter to make shapes.

3   Place the oat cakes on a baking tray and bake for about 20 minutes until golden brown. I defy you to wait until they've cooled down before you're spreading one with butter...

Shutterstock/Marilyn Barbone

Traditional Orange Marmalade

Thanks go to Shirley Spear, chef/owner of the fabulous Three Chimneys Restaurant on the Isle of Skye for this recipe; the marmalade is used later in the book in her simple but delicious hot marmalade pudding.

Ingredients

2 kg Seville oranges

4 lemons

4 kg granulated sugar

4 ltrs water

Method

1   Put the whole fruit in a basin of very lukewarm water and give them a good wash and a gentle scrub. Put the washed fruit, whole, into a large saucepan or preserving pan. Add the water and put the lid on. Bring to the boil and simmer for about one-and-a-half hours. You should be able to easily pierce the skins of the fruit easily with a skewer when they are ready. Remove the fruit from the water and place on a large dish to cool down a little.

2   With a sharp knife, cut the cooked fruit into quarters and scrape out the pulp and pips.

3   Add the pips, the pulp and any obvious residual juice, into the pan with the water that was used to boil the fruit. Boil the pips and pulp for a full 10 minutes and then strain through a sieve.

4   Keep the juice, but discard the strained pulp and pips.

5   Meanwhile, put the sugar in a large flat container, roasting dish or bowl and
     put it into a low oven to warm through. This will make it easier for the sugar
     to dissolve. Chop or slice the orange and lemon peel to your favourite size
     and shape. Do this by hand with a sharp cook's knife rather than in a food
     processor. If the rind is too pulpy it makes cloudy marmalade.

6   Put your clean jam jars into the low oven to warm through ready for potting
     the marmalade.

7   Butter the base of your pan with a thin skim of unsalted butter. This prevents
     the marmalade from sticking to the base of the pan when it is cooking.

8   Put the strained water into the pan together with the chopped peel. Bring to
     the boil slowly.

9   Turn down the heat. Add the warm sugar. Stir over a gentle heat until you
     are sure that all the sugar is dissolved. Bring this mixture to the boil and
     continue to boil rapidly (a "rolling boil") without stirring for approximately half
     an hour. You are aiming to reach setting point. To test for setting point put a
     small spoonful onto a very cold saucer. (Keep a few at the ready in the fridge
     or freezer) Allow it to cool a little and then push it with your finger, or tilt the
     dish to one side. If the marmalade wrinkles up, it is ready.

10   Leave the marmalade in the hot pan for a
     short time until it shows that it is beginning to
     set properly. The peel will be showing signs
     of becoming "suspended" in the mixture.
     Carefully ladle the hot marmalade into warm,
     clean jars. Seal the finished jars.

**Shutterstock/
Marilyn Barbone**

Carrot & Orange Soup

At certain times of the year (I'm talking about the depths of winter) we need comfort and a bit of colour in our lives. This robust, simple soup has both in ladles. It also has the added bonus of making the kitchen smell heavenly.

Ingredients SERVES 4

25g butter

750g fresh tomatoes, chopped

100g red lentils

1 large onions, chopped

1 medium carrot, chopped

1 large orange

Bay leaf

900ml stock (make your own - see page 6) or use Marigold Boullion

Sea salt

Freshly ground black pepper

Method

1   Heat the butter in a large pan. Add the onions, carrot and lentils and cook gently for five minutes. Peel the rind off the orange with a spud peeler, slice it finely and add it to the pan with the tomatoes and bay leaf.

2   Pour in the stock, season and bring to the boil. Cover and simmer for an hour. Remove the bay leaf and blitz. Add the orange juice; serve with or without a swirl of cream but with a hunk of home made soda bread (see page 8).

Shutterstock/Joerg Benge

Cheese and Thyme Tarts

These tasty tarts are simple to make and easy on the purse. Eat them warm or cold — either way you can't fail to impress the family or dinner guests.

Ingredients

Packet ready-made short crust pastry (or make your own)

1 onion, thinly sliced

1 red pepper, thinly sliced

150g strong, hard grated cheese

120ml double cream

1 medium egg

1 sprig thyme, leaves removed and finely chopped

Sea salt and freshly ground black pepper

Method

1   Pre-heat the oven to 190C/370F/gas 1. Roll out the pastry to the thickness of a pound coin on a lightly floured surface. Line the pastry cases then top with a disk of greaseproof paper and baking beans. Cook for 10 minutes. Remove the paper and beans and cook for a further 5 minutes. Remove and cool.

To make the filling

2   Gently fry the onion and red pepper in a tablespoon of olive oil until they're soft but not brown. Divide between the four cases. Crumble the cheese on top of the onions. Whisk the cream and egg together, add the thyme, season and pour into the cases. Cook in the middle of the oven for 15 minutes (the pastry will be a lovely golden brown and the cheese mix bubbling). Serve hot or cold with a green salad and a fat slice of brown bread.

©Joan Ransley

Cullen Skink

This hearty, tasty soup is a firm favourite in our house; the smoked fish and soft potatoes with the addition of cream never fails to comfort, even on the darkest winter's night. It may or may not have originated on the Moray Firth, but its popularity all over the country isn't in question.

Ingredients SERVES 6

500g undyed smoked haddock, skin on

A bay leaf

Knob of butter

4 shallots, peeled & finely chopped

2 medium potatoes, peeled, cut into chunks

500ml whole milk

100ml white wine

90ml double cream

Freshly ground black pepper

Chives, chopped, to serve

Method

1. Put the fish into a pan large enough to hold it comfortably, and cover with about 300ml cold milk. Add the bay leaf, and bring gently to a simmer for about 5 minutes. Remove from the pan, and set aside to cool. Take the pan off the heat, keeping the milk.

2. Melt the butter in another pan on a medium-low heat, and add the shallots. Cook without colouring (stir from time to time) for about 10 minutes until softened. Season generously with black pepper.

3. Add the potato and stir to coat with butter. Pour in the haddock cooking liquor and bay leaf, and bring to a simmer. Cook until the potato is tender.

Shutterstock/MB Images

4. Meanwhile, remove the skin, and any bones from the haddock, and break into flakes.

5. Add the remaining milk, wine, cream and haddock to the pan and simmer for another 5 minutes. Discard the bay leaf.

6. Check the seasoning, adding a pinch of salt if required (you won't need much; the smoked fish is quite salty). Serve with a generous spoonful of the potato, leek and haddock mixture in each bowl, and a sprinkling of chives.

Smoked venison and Wild Mushroom Toast

Mhairi Robertson from the Rannoch Smokery in Perthshire has very kindly allowed me to use this super recipe; it's incredibly easy and completely delicious. It works well as a dinner party starter or a supper – either way, with a glass of fruity red wine it's a winner. There's no shop at the smokery but the fabulous House of Bruar on the A9 just north of Pitlochry sell their full range; the award-winning dry-cured wild Scottish venison used here is just one of their mouthwatering products.

Ingredients SERVES 2

1 pack of Rannoch sliced smoked venison

200g wild mushrooms (large flat field mushrooms will do)

1 tbsp olive oil

2 shallots, peeled and thinly sliced

1 clove garlic, thinly sliced

1 tsp rosemary, finely chopped

1 tbsp whisky

2 tbsp mascarpone

Sea salt

Freshly ground black pepper

4 slices fat baguette, toasted

Method

1   Heat the oil in a frying pan and throw in the mushrooms when the oil is hot. Stir fry for about five minutes then remove to a plate. Lower the heat and add the shallots and garlic.

2   Cook gently for five minutes until softened then add the rosemary and cook for a further minute. Add the whisky, and mascarpone and bubble to reduce.

3   Place the toast on a baking tray, top each piece with slices of smoked venison then a pile of the mushroom mixture. Place under a hot grill for a minute or so, until it bubbles. Voila!

©Rannoch Smokery

Smoked Salmon Paté

You can buy it from the supermarket of course, but making your own pate is much more satisfying and as easy as ABC. It's particularly lovely with a slice of home made soda bread (see page 8).

Ingredients

250g smoked salmon

110g cream cheese

2 tbsp whipping cream

1 tbsp lemon juice

Sea salt

Freshly ground black pepper

Chopped chives

Method

1   Put the smoked salmon and cream cheese in a blender and whizz it until you've got a smooth mix.

2   Remove from the processor and put in a bowl. Add the lemon juice, the lightly whipped cream and chives and mix well. Chill for about half an hour before serving. Serve with a chunk of bread and a quarter of lemon to squeeze over.

Shutterstock/Martin Turzak

Beetroot and goats cheese salad

This is a stunningly robust salad, full of earthiness and sweetness. Any soft cheese will do but goat's cheese works particularly well; creamy, nutty Ailsa Craig (named after the island just off the Southern Ayrshire coast) is the perfect ingredient. If you choose to cook the beetroot from scratch, allow an hour in the oven (having wrapped them first in aluminium foil) but vacuum-packed cooked beets do the job just as well.

Ingredients SERVES 4

6 medium sized cooked beetroots (room temperature)

250g crumbly cheese

For the dressing

2 tbsp white wine vinegar

½ tsp Dijon mustard

5 tbsp olive oil

1 tsp caraway seeds

Sea salt and freshly ground black pepper

Slices of home made bread to serve (see page 8)

Method

1   Mix together the vinegar, mustard and seasoning. Beat the olive oil in with a whisk, bit by bit. Toast the caraway seeds lightly under the grill then add them to the dressing.

2   Shred the beetroot, add the dressing, crumble the cheese into chunks and scatter through the beets. Serve with thick slices of home made bread (see page 8).

©Joan Ransley

Country Egg Casserole

This is one of those dishes I turn to time and time again (usually when I've run out of ideas); I've often got the ingredients and it's a doddle to make. There's something luxurious about it – the egg custard lifts it above being a come-day go-day vegetable stew. It's a great way of getting kids who won't eat their five a day get at least three down their necks.

Ingredients SERVES 6

Medium cauliflower, divided into florets

450g leeks, cut into thin slices

200g broccoli or green beans

185g grated cheese

6 eggs

300ml single cream

Sea salt

Freshly ground black pepper

One teaspoon mustard

Method

1   Cook the prepared vegetables in salted, boiling water for ten minutes or so. Butter the inside of a large, lidded casserole dish and add the hot vegetables to it with most of the cheese mixed in.

2   Whisk the eggs lightly with the cream and seasoning and pour over the vegetables. Sprinkle the rest of the cheese on top. Cover the casserole and bake at 180C/Gas Mark 4 for 25/30 minutes until the egg custard is set.

©Joan Ransley

Roast Rack of Lamb
with herb crust and
minty Hollandaise Sauce

This recipe is from legendary cook Claire Macdonald who has authored many cookery books and runs the cookery school at the stunning Kinloch Lodge on the Isle of Skye. She says 'I have seen – and bought – racks of lamb for sale in butcher's departments of supermarkets and they are so convenient, especially when there are only a few of you for lunch – they cook much more quickly than a large leg of lamb.' It takes a bit of time and effort but is absolutely worth it.

Ingredients SERVES 6

For the rack of lamb:

3 racks of lamb, trimmed

175g pinhead oatmeal

30 or so grinds black pepper

1 level tsp flaky salt

1 tbsp olive oil

For the minty hollandaise sauce:

300ml white wine vinegar

2 slices onion

1 tsp black peppercorns

2 bay leaves

A few parsley stalks, crushed

½ tsp salt

4 large egg yolks

220g butter, cut into small bits

2 tbsp mint, finely chopped

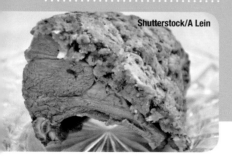
Shutterstock/A Lein

Method

1   Trim excess fat off each rack of lamb. In a bowl, mix together the pinhead oatmeal, pepper and salt with the olive oil. Put the trimmed racks of lamb in to a roasting tin lined with baking parchment – this just makes washing up so much easier afterwards – and cover each rack with the oatmeal mixture, as evenly as you can.

2   Roast in a hot oven, 200C or gas mark 6, for 15 minutes. This will give you fairly rare meat. If you – as I do – prefer lamb pink rather than red, then leave it for a bit longer. To serve, either slice each rack in half, or slice into individual chops and arrange on a warm serving plate.

1   **For the sauce:** Put the wine vinegar, onion, black peppercorns, bay leaves, parsley stalks and salt into a small saucepan and simmer till the liquid is reduced by half.

2   Meanwhile, put a saucepan containing water on to simmer and be sure that you have a Pyrex bowl that fits snugly into the pan. Using a flat whisk, beat the yolks in the Pyrex bowl, put the bowl on top of the pan of simmering water and beat the bits of butter into the yolks, a bit at a time, not adding the next bit until the previous bit has melted. You will get a thick emulsion of yolks and butter in the bowl.

3   When all the butter is incorporated, strain in about 1 tablespoon of the flavoured and reduced wine vinegar and mix it in well – the vinegar must still be hot. Taste and add more if you like a sharper flavour to the sauce. Take the bowl off the pan and pour the thick hollandaise sauce into a thermos flask to keep it warm and to allow you to wash up the saucepan, bowl and flat whisk. Before serving, stir the chopped mint into the sauce – if you add the mint too soon, it turns an unattractive brownish colour. Serve in a warmed bowl.

Fisherman's Pie

There's nowhere in Scotland more than 50 miles from the sea so fresh fish has always been central to the Scottish diet. This simple, family-friendly recipe calls for white and smoked fish – and if you're feeling flush, a handful of large prawns elevates it to a dinner party cracker. One of the great things about this recipe is that you don't have to cook the fish before you build the dish. The jury's out whether or not grated cheese goes on top; it's entirely up to you, no-one's judging you.

Ingredients SERVES 4

1 tbsp olive oil

1 leek, thinly sliced*

30g flour

300ml milk

125g prawns

Sea salt

Freshly ground black pepper

60g smoked haddock fillets

60g white fish

3 large potatoes, peeled and thinly sliced

Method

1. Pre-heat the oven to 200C/gas 6. Heat the oil over a medium heat. Add the leeks and fry for 2-3 minutes, until soft but not brown. Add the flour, stir well and cook for 1-2 minutes.

2. Remove the pan from the heat and gradually stir in the milk. Return to the heat and cook, stirring constantly until the sauce thickens. Simmer gently for five minutes.

3. Stir in the prawns and season well with salt & pepper. Place half the sauce in the pie dish. Place the fish fillets on top then spoon over the remaining sauce. Top with the sliced potato and season some more.

4. Place the dish on a baking sheet and bake for 35-40 minutes, until the potatoes are golden.

5. Serve with garden peas, broad beans or mange tout.

   *a foolproof way to make sure you've got all the grit out between the layers of leek is to put them into cold salted water for 10 minutes.

Shutterstock/stocksolutions

Tweed Kettle

A deeply traditional Scottish dish, this is sometimes called Salmon Hash and graced dining tables in the 19th century. A classic dish of salmon with white wine and shallot sauce it's quite sophisticated and goes down a storm at dinner parties. The Tweed is one of Scotland's premier salmon rivers and though this dish originates in Edinburgh it's been named in its honour.

Ingredients SERVES 4

900g fresh salmon

2 chopped shallots

Sea salt

Freshly ground black pepper

150ml water

150ml dry white wine

2 tbsp butter

115g mushrooms, chopped

Pinch of ground mace

1 tbsp flat leaf parsley

Method

1   Put the fish in a large pan (if you've got a fish kettle, this is the time to dust it down) just covered with water and bring to the boil. Simmer gently for five minutes. Remove fish from the pan, keeping the stock; remove skin and bone and cut the fish into bite-size squares.

2   Season with salt, pepper and mace and put into a clean dish with a quarter pint of the fish stock plus the wine and finely chopped shallot or chives. Cover the dish and simmer gently for about 20 minutes.

3   Heat up the butter and soften the mushrooms in it, drain and add to the salmon and heat together for another five minutes. Serve with chopped parsley. Traditionally this dish is served with mashed swede or potatoes.

Shutterstock/Tatiana Vorona

Finnan Haddie

James Boswell wrote about smoked fish in the 18th century (observing that it could be bought in London) but there are references to this delicious Scottish delicacy as far back at the 16th century. Findon (locally known as 'Finnan') a fishing village in Aberdeen began producing lightly smoked haddock (haddies) 100 years later and it became a firm favourite all over the country.

They're lovely simply grilled, but I prefer to use them to make this creamy dish – my family are mad for it.

Ingredients SERVES 4

500g smoked haddock

1 large onion, thinly sliced

2 bay leaves

400ml milk

Freshly ground black pepper

Pinch of nutmeg

30g softened butter

2 tsp plain flour

2 spring onions, finely chopped

Flat leaf parsley

Method

1   Put the thinly onions sliced in the bottom of a large saucepan with the
     bay leaves. Cut the fish into pieces about an inch wide and place over the
     onions. Add the milk and pour over the fish. Grind in a good teaspoon
     of pepper. Bring gently to the boil then reduce the heat and simmer,
     covered, for about five minutes. Take the lid off and simmer for a further
     five minutes.

2   With a slotted spoon
     remove the fish and put
     in a warm serving dish.
     Continue to simmer the
     milk in the pan for another
     five minutes, stirring
     continuously. Blend the
     warm butter and flour
     together and add to the
     pan along with the finely
     chopped spring onion. Stir
     over a low heat until the
     mixture thickens then add
     the nutmeg.

3   Pour over the fish and
     sprinkle the parsley over
     the top. This is quite a rich
     dish so I usually serve it
     with plain boiled potatoes.

Shutterstock/Daniel Gilbey Photography

Scottish Beef Casserole with dumplings

Scotland produces some of the best beef in the world; Aberdeen Angus is arguably the best known breed, renowned for the rich and tasty flavour of the meat. Everyone has their own version of this classic dish; a long, slow cook brings the taste out of all the component parts of this rib-sticking winter warmer. Beer-wise, there are dozens of large and micro-breweries up and down the country; choose any dark, sweet variety here.

Ingredients SERVES 4-6

1 tbsp sunflower oil

750g beef shin, stewing steak or skirt

4 small onions, peeled and diced

4 carrots, peeled and diced

2 celery stalks, diced

3 bay leaves

2 tbsp Worcestershire Sauce

500ml bottle beer

Sea salt and freshly ground black pepper

For the dumplings

175g self raising flour

75g shredded suet

Salt & pepper

1 tsp dried thyme

Cold water

Method

1. Warm the oil in a large casserole pot. Add the meat and let it brown slightly, then remove and keep warm. Add the onions and cook until they're transparent but not brown; add the rest of the vegetables and sweat for 5 minutes. Put the meat back then add the beer, tomatoes, Worcestershire Sauce, bay leaves and seasoning. Put the lid on and simmer for about 1 ½ hours.

For the dumplings

2. Sift the flour into a bowl then add the suet, seasoning and thyme. Add about 5 tbsp cold water, mix together till you have a soft, slightly sticky dough. Flour your hands and put the dough on a floured surface. Shape the dough into a big ball then cut up into about 8 balls. Drop the dumplings into the stew and cook with the lid off for a further 15 minutes until they're plump and moist.

3. Serve straight from the pot with crusty bread to soak up the gravy!

Shutterstock/Paul Cowan

Abernethy Biscuits

Abernethy is a small town in Perthshire but history has it that their roots belong to a Dr Abernethy who suggested the addition of caraway seeds and sugar to plain biscuits. Wherever the truth lies, there's no doubt that they pass the taste test, in any home.

Ingredients

225g plain flour

1/2 tsp baking powder

85g butter

85g granulated sugar

1/2 tsp caraway seeds

Standard egg, lightly beaten

1 tbsp milk

Method

1 Sift the flour and baking powder into a bowl. Rub the butter in until you've got a consistency like breadcrumbs. Add the sugar and caraway seeds then add the egg and milk to make a stiff dough.

2 Roll the mixture onto a floured surface until it's about 1/2" thick. Cut shapes out with a cookie cutter. Prick the top of the biscuits with a form and place on a greased baking tray. Bake in a pre-heated oven at 190C/gas 5 for ten minutes until they're a light golden brown.

Shutterstock/Dream79

Dundee Cake

This rich, dense cake became popular at the end of the 19th century and is a delicious alternative to Christmas cake – less rich and moist, more crumbly. Legend has it that Mary Queen of Scots wasn't a fan of cherries so the cake was made for her with almonds instead. If it's good enough for her...

Ingredients

225g plain flour

1 level teaspoon baking powder

170g butter

140g golden caster sugar

4 eggs

45g mixed peel

170g each of currants, raisins, sultanas

Grated rind and juice of lemon

2 tablespoons whisky

2 tablespoons boiled milk and 1 tablespoon sugar

30g blanched almonds

Method

1   Sift the flour and baking powder into a large mixing bowl. Add the butter, caster sugar and lightly beaten eggs then combine with an electric hand whisk for a couple of minutes until you have a smooth batter. If it seems too dry, add a dessertspoon of milk.

2   Fold in all the other ingredients: currants, sultanas, mixed peel, ground almonds, whisky and lemon zest. Spoon the mixture into the prepared cake tin, spreading it out evenly with the back of the spoon. Put the whole almonds in concentric circles over the top.

3   Place the cake near the centre of the oven and bake for 1¾ hours or until the centre is firm and springy to touch. Allow it to cool before taking it out of the tin.

4   You don't need to wait for Christmas – this cake is delicious all year round, particularly with a cup of tea in front of the fire!

Shutterstock/MB Images

Cranachan

This seriously boozy dessert is a traditional Scottish dish and a great alternative to trifle. It's really simple to make (no actual cooking) and absolutely delicious – your dinner guests will be impressed!

Ingredients SERVES 4

550ml double cream

85g porridge oats

7tbsp whisky

3 tbsp runny honey

450g raspberries or strawberries

Fresh mint, to garnish

Method

1   Toast the oats in a frying pan. Lightly whip the cream until it stands in soft peaks then fold in the whisky, honey, oatmeal and berries.

2   Serve in dessert glasses garnished with a few berries and mint leaves.

Shutterstock/al1962

Hot Marmalade Pudding

This crowd-pleasing steamed pudding was created 30 years ago by Shirley Spear, chef-owner of the fabulous Three Chimneys on the Isle of Skye. It's been on the menu since they opened in 1984 – no wonder, it's delicious. Made with breadcrumbs and only a little flour it's beautifully light. Serve it with cream, custard or ice cream and watch your family faint with delight.

Ingredients

50g fine brown breadcrumbs

120g soft light brown sugar

25g self-raising flour

120g butter

8 tbsp good course cut marmalade (see page 16)

3 large eggs

1 tsp bicarbonate of soda

1 tbsp water

Method

1   Butter a 3 pint pudding basin. Put the breadcrumbs, flour and sugar in a large mixing bowl. Melt the butter with the marmalade over a gentle heat.

2   Pour the melted ingredients over the dry ingredients and mix together well. Whisk the eggs until frothy and beat gently into the mixture until blended together thoroughly.

3   Finally, dissolve the bicarb in 1 tbsp of cold water. Stir this into the pudding mixture – it will increase in volume – as if by magic!

4   Spoon the mixture into the prepared pudding basin and cover it with a close fitting lid or make one with circles of buttered greaseproof paper and foil which you then tie around the rim of the basin.

5   Put the basin in a saucepan of boiling water (the water should reach half way up the side). Cover the pan with a close-fitting lid and simmer for two hours. The water will need topping up now and again.

6   Turn out onto a serving dish, slice and serve hot with fresh cream, ice cream or custard.

Potato Scones

Many traditional Scottish recipes use ingredients which were simple to source and light on the wallet; these delicious, easy to make savoury scones don't last five minutes in this house.

Ingredients

225g boiled and mashed potatoes

65g flour

3 tbsp melted butter

½ tsp salt

85g grated cheese (optional)

Olive oil for cooking

Method

1   Mash the potatoes while they're warm and add the butter and salt. Sift in enough flour to make a pliable dough. Turn out onto a floured surface and roll until about ¼ inch thick.

2   Use a scone cutter. Prick with a fork. Warm a tablespoon of olive oil in a large pan and cook the scones – three minutes each side should do the trick. A tasty addition is a sprinkling of grated farmhouse cheese on the top of each scone.

Shutterstock/photoline

Scotch Eggs

Home made scotch eggs couldn't be further from the shop-bought variety, in the sense that they're very tasty! They might be a bit fiddly but I can guarantee they're worth it. We eat these almost every week in summer – either at the table with a sharp green salad – or of course they're perfect picnic food.

Ingredients SERVES 4

4 large free range eggs

275g sausage meat

1 sprig fresh rosemary, leaves removed and chopped

1 sprig fresh sage, leaves removed and chopped

1 tsp sweet paprika

Nutmeg

Sea salt

Freshly ground black pepper

125g plain flour, seasoned with salt & pepper

1 medium egg, beaten

125g white breadcrumbs

Vegetable oil for deep frying

Method

1   Put the eggs in a pan of cold salted water and bring to the boil. Reduce the heat to a simmer and cook for nine 10 minutes. Drain and cool the eggs under cold running water, then peel.

2   Mix the sausage meat with the herbs in a bowl and season generously with salt & pepper. Divide the sausage meat mixture into four and flatten each one out into ovals on a lightly floured surface. Put the seasoned flour in a dish and roll each egg in it before wrapping the meat around them.

3   Dip each sausage meat covered egg in beaten egg then dip the egg in breadcrumbs. Heat the oil in a deep pan until a small piece of bread crust sizzles and turns brown. Carefully place each egg into the hot oil and deep fry for about 10 minutes, until they're crisp and golden. Carefully remove with a slatted spoon and drain on kitchen paper.

4   Serve cool with a simply dressed green salad or put them in the fridge ready to take on your picnic!

Shutterstock/Razmarinka

Kedgeree

The origins of this deeply satisfying dish can be traced back to the 14th century as an Indian rice and bean dish, Khichri, but it's perhaps more widely known as a breakfast staple during the British Raj in India and brought back to the UK by returning colonials. It's more often eaten at tea time now – but if you want to evoke the Raj vibe, go ahead and have it before you leave for the office! Smoked haddock from Glen Finnan in the Highlands works beautifully, but any smoked fish will do.

Ingredients SERVES 4

2 fillets smoked haddock, bones & skin removed

2 hard boiled eggs, shelled and finely chopped

350g basmati rice

300ml milk

50g butter

600ml stock (see page 6)

Small onion, finely chopped

Bay leaf

1 tsp turmeric

1 tsp ground coriander

1 tsp curry powder

Sea salt

Freshly ground black pepper

Fresh coriander

Method

1 Heat the oil in a large, lidded pan, add the onion and gently fry for 5 minutes until softened but not coloured. Add the spices, season with salt, then continue to fry until the mix start to go brown and fragrant; about 3 minutes.

2 Add the rice and stir in well. Add the stock, stir then bring to the boil. Reduce to a simmer then cover for 10 minutes. Take off the heat and leave to stand, covered, for 10-15 minutes more. The rice will be perfectly cooked if you do not lift the lid before the end of the cooking.

3 Meanwhile, put the haddock and bay leaves in a frying pan, cover with the milk then poach for 10 minutes until the flesh flakes. Remove from the milk, peel away the skin, then flake the flesh into bite-size pieces.

4 Put the eggs in a pan, cover with water, bring to the boil then reduce to a simmer. Leave for 4½-5 minutes plunge into cold water, then peel and cut the eggs into quarters. Gently mix the fish, eggs, parsley, coriander and rice together in the pan. Serve hot, sprinkled with fresh coriander.

Shutterstock/travellight

Arbroath Smokies on Toast with Cheese

Traditionally produced in small family smokehouses on the east coast fishing town of Arbroath, 'smokies' are whole wood-smoked haddock with the backbone still intact. You'll know when you're eating the genuine article; the piquant taste is quite unique. The skin of the fish has a coppery brown colour and the flesh is creamy with a rich, smoky flavour – perfect for this tea time treat.

Ingredients SERVES 4

175g smoked haddock

175ml milk

5g plain flour

25g strong, hard, grated cheese

One egg (separated into white and yolk)

Sea salt

Freshly ground black pepper

4 slices of buttered toast

Method

1   Heat the smoked haddock in 150ml of the milk in a saucepan. Bring to the boil, reduce the heat, cover and cook gently for about five minutes or until the fish flakes easily with a fork. Remove the fish and flake it with a fork.

2   To make a white sauce, make a roux with the flour with the rest of the milk in a small pan. Add the fishy milk and heat gently, stirring all the time – it should take a couple of minutes to thicken up. Stir in the cheese, egg yolk and flaked fish.

3   Season to taste with salt and freshly ground black pepper, then heat through. Whisk the egg white until it is stiff and fold in with a metal spoon.

4   Grill the toast then spoon the fish mixture onto each slice. Put it back under a hot grill until it's lightly browned. Serve immediately.

Shutterstock/Alex Helin

Leek & Potato Soup

This simple, hearty soup is popular throughout Scotland; it's good enough to make double the quantity and batch freeze it. It's beautifully creamy without being hugely calorific.

Ingredients SERVES 4

6 potatoes, peeled and diced

3 leeks, cut into slices about the width of a pound coin

25g butter

750ml stock (see page 6)

Sea salt

Freshly ground black pepper

Pinch of ground nutmeg

Chopped chives for garnish

Method

1   Boil the potatoes for about
    20 minutes, until they're soft
    but not mushy. In a large
    heavy based pot melt the
    butter and add the cleaned
    leeks. Cook for around 10
    minutes, until the leeks are
    transparent, not brown.

2   Add the drained potatoes, the
    stock and seasoning. Cook
    gently for about 10 minutes
    until all the vegetables are
    nicely soft. Some folk like to
    whizz it smooth in a blender,
    others like the chunks. It's
    entirely up to you.

3   Ladle into warm bowls and
    chop the fresh chives on the
    top. Serve with home made
    bread (see page 8).

Shutterstock/travellight

Colcannon

This hearty, economical dish originated in Ireland but it's been eaten the length and breadth of Scotland for centuries; in the Borders it's known as Rumbledethumps and in Aberdeenshire, Kailkenny. There are several variations include adding a couple of boiled and mashed carrots and turnips, and sometimes cream is used instead of butter. Regardless of which additions you choose you can be sure that the family will rush to the table and polish off the lot.

Ingredients

450g potatoes

450g cabbage

30g butter

Sea salt and freshly ground black pepper

Method

1   Boil and mash the potatoes. Boil the cabbage then finely chop it. Mix in a large saucepan in which the butter has been melted. Keep the saucepan over a low heat to keep it hot. Season to taste and serve piping hot.

2   The mixture can also be put into a greased oven-proof dish and cooked at 200C/gas mark 6 until the top is browned.

Shutterstock/Monkey Business Images

Scottish Rarebit

What makes this simple, delicious lunch or tea time favourite different from the classic Welsh rarebit is the addition of strong, nutty but sweet Isle of Mull farmhouse cheese and local craft beer. Hundreds of breweries have sprung up all over Scotland in the last 20 years - so take your pick – but I can recommend Terror of Tobermory from the Isle of Mull Brewing Company – it's nicely fruity!

Ingredients

4 slices thick bread, brown or white

2 tbsp plain flour

900g Isle of Mull cheese, crumbled

2 tsp English mustard powder

1 tsp cayenne pepper

400ml bottled beer

Generous splash Worcestershire Sauce

80g butter

Method

1   Gently melt the butter in a small, heavy-based saucepan. Gently whisk in the flour, mustard and cayenne pepper. Add the beer and Worcestershire Sauce, whisking all the time. Add the crumbled cheese, stirring until it's all melted.

2   Take off the heat and let it cool completely while you toast the bread. Pour the cheese mix over the toast then put under a hot grill until the whole thing is bubbling and golden.

©Joan Ransley

Store Cupboard Staples

Worcestershire Sauce
Marigold Swiss Vegetable
Bouillon
Kallo stock cubes
Wholemeal flour
Plain white flour
Self raising flour
Granulated sugar
Soft light brown sugar
Golden caster sugar
Instant yeast
Bicarbonate of soda
Baking powder
Miniature bottle of whisky
Red lentils

Dried thyme
Olive oil
Vegetable oil
Bay leaves
Tinned chopped tomatoes
English mustard powder
Dijon mustard
Wholegrain mustard
Ground cumin
Ground coriander
Ground turmeric
Ground mace
Ground nutmeg
Caraway seeds
Curry powder

Cayenne pepper
Chilli flakes
Black peppercorns
Sea salt (Maldon is the
best, but any will do)
Ready made
Short crust pastry
White wine vinegar
Tomato passata
Sweet paprika
Jar of runny honey

About
Amanda Wragg

Amanda Wragg is a freelance food and feature writer, born in Derbyshire and now based near Hebden Bridge on the Pennines. She writes for the Yorkshire Post, Alastair Sawday, Square Meal and the AA. She sits on several judging panels for regional and national food & drink awards, inspects and writes for a well-known restaurant review publication and co-writes a website dedicated to good places to eat and stay in Yorkshire,
www.squidbeak.co.uk

About
Joan Ransley

Joan Ransley is a food photojournalist based in Ilkley, West Yorkshire. She works for local and national publications including The Yorkshire Post, Yorkshire Life, Derbyshire Life, The University of Leeds, The Guardian and the online Travel Magazine – Food Tripper. Joan is a member of the Guild of Food Writers.
www.joanransley.co.uk